NUTS

Designed by Eddie Goldfine
Culinary editing by Tamar Zakut
Layout by Ariane Rybski
Edited by Sorelle Weinstein
Photography by Danya Weiner
Nutritional Information by Rachel Granot, B.S., M.P.H.

Library of Congress Cataloging-in-Publication Data

Laskin, Avner.
Nuts : more than 75 delicious & healthy recipes / Avner Laskin ; photography by Danya Weiner.
p. cm.
Includes index.
ISBN-13: 978-1-4027-4469-3
ISBN-10: 1-4027-4469-2
1. Cookery (Nuts) I. Title.
TX814.L38 2008
641.6'45--dc22   2007012946

2 4 6 8 10 9 7 5 3 1

Published by Sterling Publishing Co., Inc.
387 Park Avenue South, New York, NY 10016
© 2008 by Penn Publishing Ltd.
Distributed in Canada by Sterling Publishing
c/o Canadian Manda Group, 165 Dufferin Street,
Toronto, Ontario, Canada M6K 3H6
Distributed in the United Kingdom by GMC Distribution Services,
Castle Place, 166 High Street, Lewes, East Sussex, England BN7 1XU
Distributed in Australia by Capricorn Link (Australia) Pty. Ltd.
P.O. Box 704, Windsor, NSW 2756, Australia

Printed in China
All rights reserved

Sterling ISBN-13: 978-1-4027-4469-3
ISBN-10: 1-4027-4469-2

For information about custom editions, special sales, premium and
corporate purchases, please contact Sterling Special Sales
Department at 800-805-5489 or specialsales@sterlingpub.com.

AVNER LASKIN

NUTS

More than 75 Delicious
& Healthy Recipes

PHOTOGRAPHY BY DANYA WEINER

STERLING

New York / London
www.sterlingpublishing.com

TABLE OF CONTENTS

ALL ABOUT NUTS

INTRODUCTION

Why nuts? Almond, Brazil nut, cashew, chestnut, coconut, corn nut, hazelnut, macadamia, peanut, pine nut, pistachio, walnut. A better question is, "Why not?" Nuts have been a basic part of culinary history for thousands of years. Nuts are versatile, healthy, and, luckily for chefs, absolutely delicious. Nut oils are perfect for cooking with because of their strong flavor and relatively high smoke point. These qualities make nut oils ideal for use in frying foods and produce lighter, healthier dishes.

What are nuts, exactly? Scientifically speaking, in botanical terms, a nut is the dried fruit of a plant whose ovary wall hardens as it matures and does not fuse with the seed. In cooking, however, the term "nuts" refers to many things which are actually seeds. In fact, many of the common ingredients we call nuts, such as almonds, cashews, and pistachios, are seeds. There are as many uses for nuts and seeds as there are varieties. Nuts are wonderful in pasta and salads, and of course, baking with nuts produces delicious results.

This book contains more than 85 recipes that showcase the versatility of nuts. In **Spreads and Sauces**, you will find recipes for tasty sandwich toppers, as well as sauces and salad dressings. **Vegetables and Salads** provides wonderful ways to use nuts in healthy salads and savory vegetable dishes. **Baked Goods** will teach you how to incorporate nuts into many types of breads and savory pastries. Of course, no cookbook about nuts would be complete without a chapter on **Baked Treats**. In **Hot Dishes**, you'll find out how nuts can enhance the flavor of your entrées. And finally, **Desserts** contains some restaurant-quality recipes as a fitting end to our exploration of nuts.

Bon Appétit,

Avner Laskin

TYPES OF NUTS IN THIS BOOK

In the recipes in this book, I use the nuts that I think are most appropriate and most delicious for each recipe. However, the kitchen is the place for experimentation and individual expression. If you dislike a particular nut in a recipe, try a different type. You may be pleasantly surprised and may even find a new family favorite.

Walnuts – There are 59 varieties of walnut tree. The meat of the walnut is wrinkled and oily, and it has a strong flavor that is perfect for a wide variety of recipes.

Almonds – Almonds come either shelled or unshelled, and sweet or bitter. For cooking, it is preferable to use sweet, shelled almonds. Blanched almonds are better for baking.

Chestnuts – For me, chestnuts symbolize winter. I love to use them shelled and roasted, in dishes that have rich sauces, and for fancy desserts. You can find chestnuts preserved, candied, roasted, canned, and even as a paste. Fresh chestnuts should be stored in a paper bag in the refrigerator.

Peanuts – Obviously, the most common use for peanuts is peanut butter. But peanuts—which are actually classified as legumes, not nuts or seeds—are as good mixed with raisins in a trail mix as they are as part of an Asian stir-fry. They can be used salted and unsalted in both sweet and savory recipes.

Cashews – These nuts are native to Brazil, which is one of the few places cashew juice is served as a drink. This nut is great for Asian cooking, with noodles, for baking, salads, and in Middle Eastern cuisine.

Pecans – Excellent in baking and cooking, the pecan is great either sweet or savory. It can be used salted or candied and is one of my favorites.

Coconuts – You either love coconuts or you hate them. Personally, I love both the taste and aroma of coconut and find that the taste of coconut in a recipe conjures images of a tropical vacation. The white fleshy part of the coconut is the part used in cooking.

Macadamia Nuts – A nut suitable for a king. The worldwide demand for macadamia nuts far exceeds the crop yield, so their price is relatively high. Macadamia nuts are great for use in sweet recipes. The macadamia can be stored for up to 2 months, refrigerated in an airtight container.

Brazil Nuts – A rich-tasting nut found in the Amazon region that is suitable for a wide variety of recipes.

Hazelnuts – Another of my personal favorites, the hazelnut is often used in confections and desserts.

Pine Nuts – Pine nuts are another versatile type of nut. They can be gently roasted and sprinkled over salads, or ground and used in pesto sauce.

Nutmeg – Primarily used as a spice, nutmeg is best stored whole and ground with a spice grater when needed.

Pistachios – The greener the pistachio, the stronger and richer the flavor. Pistachios can be used in both baking and cooking and can also be eaten roasted in the shell.

PURCHASE AND STORAGE

Nuts, like fruit, are seasonal. Therefore, they are best purchased when they are in season and best used when fresh. Purchase fresh nuts in fine groceries or in natural foods stores that sell nuts in bulk. Always purchase nuts in their shells as the shell protects the nuts from spoilage. As soon as a nut is shelled, it begins to lose its freshness. Choose nuts that are heavy for their size as a heavier nut is fresher. Fresh nuts should be stored in their shells in an airtight container to prevent moisture damage. You may also freeze shelled nuts or nuts that have cracked shells, like pistachios, to keep them fresh. Certain nuts, like pine nuts, should be stored in the refrigerator in an airtight container.

Roasting Nuts

You may wish to roast the nuts you purchase. Roasting fresh nuts, as opposed to purchasing roasted nuts, allows you to roast only the amount you need and thus maintains the freshness of purchased nuts. The process is simple—you just place the amount you wish in a baking pan and roast it in an oven that has been preheated to 300°F. The method is slightly different for each type of nut.

Hazelnut shells will crack and the meat will turn golden after 20–30 minutes. Roasting **chestnuts** requires cutting into the shells first. **Pistachios** are ready after 10 minutes in the oven.

SALTED NUTS

INGREDIENTS

Makes 1 pound salted nuts in their shells

1 pound fresh nuts, in the shell

1 tablespoon coarse salt

½ cup boiling water

PREPARATION

1. Preheat the oven to 300°F.

2. Wash the nuts well and crack their shells. It is not necessary to remove the meat. You may use a nutcracker or your hands.

3. Spread in one layer in a baking pan.

4. Dissolve the coarse salt in the boiling water and pour over the nuts.

5. Make sure that all the nuts are soaked in the salt solution.

6. Cook for 40 minutes until the nuts are dried, stirring occasionally.

SWEET NUTS

INGREDIENTS

Makes 2 cups shelled sweet nuts

¼ cup water

1 cup sugar

2 cups fresh nuts, shelled

PREPARATION

1. In a saucepan over high heat, combine the water and sugar and cook while stirring, until the sugar is completely dissolved and the liquid becomes thick. Stir until all the sugar is liquefied and there are no remaining sugar crystals.

2. Add the nuts and continue to stir to completely coat the nuts.

3. Remove from the heat and spread the nuts in one layer on baking paper.

4. Let the nuts cool completely and store in an airtight container.

NUTRITIONAL INFORMATION

Nuts are an essential part of a healthy diet. Many people believe nuts to be unhealthy and fattening. However, nutritionally, it is important to distinguish between different kinds of fats. There are "good" fats and there are "bad" fats. Nuts primarily contain the "good" kind of fats—those which help reduce the risk of heart disease, protect the blood, and help fight the effects of aging. These fats, called unsaturated fats, are found in many types of foods such as olives, avocado, fish, and of course, nuts. Many nutritional studies indicate that eating 5–6 ounces of nuts a week can reduce the risk of heart disease by up to 30 percent.

In addition to containing unsaturated fats, or heart-healthy fats, many types of nuts contain vitamins and minerals which can significantly contribute to a healthier diet. For example, walnuts are a rich source of vitamin E, an antioxidant which fights free radicals in the blood, protects against cancer, and fights the effects of aging. Walnuts are also a good source of oil; they contain Omega-3 acids, also found in fish, which can combat heart disease. Brazil nuts are an excellent source of selenium, another disease-fighter. In fact, just two Brazil nuts contain the recommended daily allowance of Selenium.

Peanuts are also wonderful sources of healthy vitamins and minerals. In addition to unsaturated fats and vitamin E, peanuts contain folic acid, which reduces the level of homocysteine in the blood. Homocysteine is increasingly being recognized as a contributor to various medical ailments, including heart disease and stroke. Finally, almonds, which contain not only unsaturated fats but also vitamins B, C, and E, are an excellent source of protein in a healthy diet.

As you can see, nuts are not only tasty, they are a perfect addition to a nutritionally sound diet. Prepare the recipes in *Nuts* and you will find inventive and fun ways to add more of these nutritious foods to your diet.

SPREADS
AND
SAUCES

NUT CHUTNEY

This tasty condiment is great as a marinade or sauce.

Serves 4

2 tablespoons canola oil

1 white onion, finely chopped

1 tablespoon garlic, finely chopped

1 cup walnuts, chopped

2 tablespoons honey

1 teaspoon ground black pepper

½ teaspoon red chili pepper, finely chopped

2 teaspoons salt

1 tablespoon sweet paprika

1 tablespoon red wine vinegar

½ pound crushed tomatoes (fresh or canned)

PREPARATION

1. Heat a heavy deep skillet over medium heat.

2. Add the oil and onion and cook for 5 minutes while stirring occasionally, until the onion is translucent.

3. Add the garlic and cook for 2 minutes.

4. Add the walnuts, mix well, and cook for 3 minutes.

5. Add the honey, black pepper, chili, salt, and paprika, and mix well. Pour the vinegar over the ingredients, mix well, and cook for 2 minutes.

6. Add the tomatoes and mix well.

7. Reduce heat and cook for 30–40 minutes until the mixture is thick.

8. Serve immediately, or transfer to an airtight container and store in the refrigerator for up to 1 week.

COCONUT CHUTNEY

Coconut flakes give this chutney an Indian flavor.

INGREDIENTS

Serves 4

2 tablespoons canola oil

1 white onion, finely chopped

1 tablespoon garlic, finely chopped

1 apple, peeled and finely chopped

2 tablespoons honey

1 teaspoon ground black pepper

½ teaspoon red chili pepper, finely chopped

1 teaspoon cinnamon

2 teaspoons salt

1 tablespoon red wine vinegar

1 cup fine coconut flakes

½ cup white wine

PREPARATION

1. Heat a heavy deep skillet over medium heat.

2. Add the oil and onion and cook for 5 minutes while stirring occasionally, until the onion is translucent.

3. Add the garlic and cook for 2 minutes.

4. Add the apple, mix well, and cook until soft and liquidy.

5. Add the honey, black pepper, chili, cinnamon, and salt, and mix well. Pour the vinegar over the ingredients and mix well. Cook for 2 minutes.

6. Add the coconut flakes and wine, and mix well. Reduce heat and cook for 10 minutes.

7. Continue to cook until the mixture is thick.

8. Remove from heat and allow to cool completely.

9. Serve when cool, or transfer to an airtight container and store in the refrigerator for up to 1 week.

SPANISH ALMOND SAUCE

Another tasty sauce that is great as a marinade or pasta sauce.

INGREDIENTS

Serves 6

½ cup roasted almonds

1 tablespoon garlic, coarsely chopped

¼ cup fresh parsley, chopped

1 small red chili pepper, seeded

2 teaspoons salt

1 teaspoon ground black pepper

2 tomatoes, blanched and quartered

1 tablespoon red wine vinegar

½ cup olive oil

PREPARATION

1. Place the almonds, garlic, parsley, chili, salt, and pepper in a food processor with a metal blade. Process until the mixture is a smooth liquid.

2. Turn off the processor, and add the tomatoes and vinegar.

3. While processing, gradually add the olive oil, and continue to process until the mixture is consistent and dark orange in color.

4. Remove the mixture with a spatula, and transfer to an airtight container.

5. Serve immediately, or store in the refrigerator for up to 2 days.

HERBED PISTACHIO SAUCE

Pour this sauce over fresh vegetables that have been briefly steamed, and you'll enjoy a light and healthy side dish.

INGREDIENTS

Serves 6

1 cup shelled pistachios

¼ cup fresh parsley

¼ cup fresh basil

1 tablespoon fresh thyme

1 tablespoon fresh oregano

1 tablespoon garlic, thickly sliced

2 teaspoons salt

1 teaspoon lemon zest

1 teaspoon ground black pepper

½ cup olive oil

2 tablespoons red wine vinegar

1 tablespoon balsamic vinegar

PREPARATION

1. Place the pistachios, parsley, basil, thyme, oregano, garlic, salt, lemon zest, and pepper in a food processor with a metal blade.

2. While processing, gradually add the oil and the vinegars, alternating between each one. Process until the sauce is almost fluorescent green and has the consistency of pesto.

3. Remove the sauce with a spatula, and transfer to an airtight container.

4. Serve immediately, or store in the refrigerator for up to 2 days.

HERBED NUT SPREAD

Perfect as a beef or chicken rub before roasting, or as a sumptuous ingredient for a hearty vegetable stew.

INGREDIENTS

Serves 4

½ cup roasted Brazil nuts

½ cup roasted walnuts

1 cup roasted pecans

1 tablespoon garlic, coarsely chopped

½ cup fresh parsley

¼ cup fresh basil

1 tablespoon fresh thyme

1 tablespoon fresh rosemary

2 teaspoons salt

1 teaspoon ground black pepper

1 tablespoon yellow mustard

½ cup olive oil

PREPARATION

1. Place all the ingredients except for the olive oil in a food processor with a metal blade.

2. While processing the mixture, gradually add the olive oil, and continue to process until smooth.

3. Remove the spread with a spatula, and transfer to an airtight container.

4. Serve immediately, or store in the refrigerator for up to 1 week.

HERBED NUT OIL

Keep this oil handy for adding to salad dressings or for marinating fresh seafood before cooking.

INGREDIENTS

Serves 4

1 red chili pepper

Peel of 1 fresh lime

1 tablespoon fresh ginger, chopped

1 tablespoon fresh garlic, chopped

1 teaspoon salt

2 pounds cold pressed nut oil (you may find this in gourmet shops or online)

PREPARATION

1. Place the chili, lime peel, ginger, garlic, and salt in a food processor with a metal blade. Process until the mixture is a smooth cream.

2. Transfer to an airtight container, and pour in the oil.

3. Serve immediately, or store in the refrigerator for up to 1 week.

SPICY NUT SPREAD

This unique spread can be mixed with pasta, added to stews, or just served on fresh bread for a tasty snack.

INGREDIENTS

Serves 4

½ cup roasted walnuts

½ cup roasted pecans

½ cup bleached almonds

1 tablespoon garlic, coarsely chopped

1 teaspoon Spanish paprika

1 tablespoon Italian seasoning

1 teaspoon salt

½ cup olive oil

PREPARATION

1. Place all the ingredients except for the olive oil in a food processor with a metal blade.

2. While processing the mixture, gradually add the olive oil, and continue to process until smooth.

3. Remove the spread with a spatula, and transfer to an airtight container.

4. Serve immediately, or store in the refrigerator for up to 1 week.

GOAT CHEESE AND NUT SPREAD

Serve this creamy spread as a dip at your next gathering, or mix it with jarred pasta sauce to make luscious lasagna.

INGREDIENTS

Serves 4

½ cup roasted walnuts

½ cup roasted pecans

½ pound fresh or slightly aged goat cheese

¼ cup fresh basil

1 tablespoon garlic, coarsely chopped

1 teaspoon salt

½ cup olive oil

PREPARATION

1. Place all the ingredients except for the olive oil in a food processor with a metal blade.

2. While processing the mixture, gradually add the olive oil, and continue to process until smooth.

3. Remove the spread with a spatula, and transfer to an airtight container.

4. Serve immediately, or store in the refrigerator for up to 1 week.

ROASTED NUT VINAIGRETTE

Spread this vinaigrette over avocado slices and serve as a tantalizing appetizer.

INGREDIENTS

Serves 4

¼ cup roasted walnuts

¼ cup roasted pecans

2 tablespoons Dijon-style mustard

1 tablespoon honey

2 teaspoons salt

1 teaspoon ground white pepper

1 cup olive oil

¼ cup red wine vinegar

PREPARATION

1. Place the walnuts, pecans, mustard, honey, salt, and pepper in a food processor with a metal blade.

2. While processing, gradually add the olive oil and vinegar, alternating between the two.

3. Process until the mixture is smooth and has the consistency of fluffy mayonnaise.

4. Remove the mixture with a spatula, and transfer to an airtight container.

5. Serve immediately, or store in the refrigerator for up to 1 week.

SPICY PEANUT BUTTER SAUCE

This spicy sauce makes a great dip for fried chicken wings.

INGREDIENTS

Serves 4

½ pound chunky peanut butter

¼ cup sweet chili sauce

1 tablespoon honey

2 tablespoons yellow mustard

1 teaspoon cayenne pepper

1 teaspoon Spanish paprika

1 teaspoon salt

1 tablespoon red wine vinegar

¼ cup canola oil

PREPARATION

1. Place the peanut butter, chili sauce, honey, mustard, pepper, paprika, and salt in a large bowl, and mix well with a metal whisk.

2. Add the vinegar and mix well.

3. Gradually add the oil while stirring. Stir until the mixture has the consistency of thick mayonnaise.

4. Transfer to an airtight container and serve immediately, or store in the refrigerator for up to 2 days.

VEGETABLES
AND
SALADS

COUSCOUS AND WALNUT SALAD

This colorful couscous salad is easy to prepare and ideal for a summer lunch.

INGREDIENTS

Serves 4

2 cups instant couscous

6 tablespoons olive oil

3 cups boiling water

½ cup walnuts, chopped

2 carrots, finely chopped

⅓ cup parsley, chopped

1 teaspoon garlic, chopped

1 tablespoon red wine vinegar

2 teaspoons salt

1 teaspoon ground white pepper

PREPARATION

1. Place the couscous and 3 tablespoons of olive oil in a large bowl. Mix well with a fork.

2. Add the boiling water, mix well, and set aside for 25 minutes.

3. Fluff the couscous with a fork and add the walnuts, carrots, parsley, garlic, vinegar, salt, pepper, and remaining olive oil.

4. Mix well and set aside for 2 hours in the refrigerator, or transfer to an airtight container for storage for up to 24 hours.

5. When it is chilled, stir the salad, transfer to serving dishes, and serve at room temperature.

VEGETABLE SALAD WITH STIR-FRIED WALNUTS AND BRAZIL NUTS

Nuoc Cham is a spicy Vietnamese sauce which, though thin and runny, contributes a rich flavor to this salad.

INGREDIENTS

Serves 6

4 carrots, cut into 2-inch-long strips, ⅛ inch thick

1 red fresh pepper, cut into thin strips

1 orange fresh pepper, cut into thin strips

1 yellow fresh pepper, cut into thin strips

2 tablespoons oil

¼ cup champignon mushrooms, thinly sliced

1 teaspoon salt

Half a white cabbage, cut into thin strips

1 tablespoon Nuoc Cham (a spicy Vietnamese dipping sauce available in gourmet stores and online)

1 tablespoon honey

¼ pound Chinese bean sprouts

½ cup roasted Brazil nuts, coarsely chopped

⅓ cup roasted walnuts, coarsely chopped

2 tablespoons soy sauce

1 tablespoon rice vinegar

⅓ cup scallions or spring onions, chopped

PREPARATION

1. Heat a wok over high heat until very hot. Add the carrots, peppers, and oil, and cook for 5 minutes while stirring.

2. Add the mushrooms and salt, and cook for 3 minutes while stirring.

3. Add the cabbage, Nuoc Cham, and honey, and cook for 3 minutes while stirring.

4. Add the sprouts, Brazil nuts, walnuts, soy sauce, and vinegar, and cook for 3 minutes while stirring.

5. Remove from heat. Add the scallions and mix well.

6. Transfer to serving plates, and serve immediately.

SEAFOOD SALAD WITH RICE NOODLES AND ROASTED PEANUTS

Use the freshest seafood you can find and you will taste the difference.

INGREDIENTS

Serves 4

1 package thin rice noodles

10 cups boiling water

½ pound shrimp, peeled, cleaned, and blanched for 4 minutes

½ pound whole calamari, Asian cut (ask for this at the seafood counter) and blanched for 4 minutes

1 teaspoon salt

½ tablespoon sesame oil

2 tablespoons Asian fish sauce

½ tablespoon fresh ginger, grated

1 red fresh pepper, cut into very thin strips

1 tablespoon rice vinegar

1 tablespoon lime juice

½ cup roasted peanuts, coarsely chopped

2 tablespoons chives, chopped

2 tablespoons fresh cilantro

PREPARATION

1. Place the noodles in a large bowl and pour in the boiling water. Let sit for 10 minutes.

2. Place the shrimp and calamari in a large bowl, and add the salt, sesame oil, fish sauce, ginger, and pepper, and mix well.

3. Drain the noodles, and transfer them to the bowl with the seafood. Add the vinegar, lime juice, peanuts, chives, and cilantro, and mix well.

4. Transfer to serving plates, and serve immediately.

WARM ROOT VEGETABLES AND WALNUT SALAD

This recipe makes a wonderful autumn or winter salad. Serve with a glass of
warm cider and enjoy a cold night indoors.

INGREDIENTS

Serves 6

3 carrots, sliced diagonally
¼ inch thick

3 parsley roots, sliced
diagonally ¼ inch thick

1 celeriac, cut in half and sliced
¼ inch thick

2 large sweet potatoes, sliced
¼ inch thick

2 beets, sliced ¼ inch thick

⅓ cup olive oil

2 teaspoons salt

⅔ cup roasted walnuts,
chopped

¼ cup parsley, chopped

1 tablespoon lemon juice,
freshly squeezed

1 teaspoon ground black
pepper

1 tablespoon red wine vinegar

PREPARATION

1. Preheat the oven to 450°F.

2. Place the carrots, parsley roots,
celeriac, sweet potatoes, beets,
half the olive oil, and 1 teaspoon
of salt in a large bowl, and mix
well. Transfer to a large deep
baking dish.

3. Bake for 30–40 minutes or
until the vegetables are soft but
not mushy.

4. Transfer the cooked vegetables
to a large serving platter.

5. Prepare the dressing. Combine
in a bowl the walnuts, parsley,
lemon juice, remaining salt,
pepper, vinegar, and remaining
olive oil. Mix well.

6. Pour the dressing over the
cooked vegetables.

7. Serve while still warm, or store
in an airtight container in the
refrigerator for up to 24 hours
and serve at room temperature.

SPROUTS AND WALNUT SALAD

Sprouts are an excellent source of antioxidants, making this salad a healthy choice.

INGREDIENTS

Serves 4

¼ cup olive oil

1 tablespoon balsamic vinegar

1 tablespoon yellow mustard

1 tablespoon honey

1 tablespoon red wine vinegar

1 teaspoon salt

1 pound assorted fresh Chinese bean sprouts (available in most grocery stores in the produce section)

½ cup roasted walnuts, coarsely chopped

½ pound cherry tomatoes, halved

½ pound Roquefort cheese or any semi-hard crumbly cheese

PREPARATION

1. Place the olive oil, balsamic vinegar, mustard, honey, red wine vinegar, and salt in a sealable jar or container, and shake well for 1 minute. Set aside.

2. Place the sprouts, walnuts, and cherry tomatoes in a large bowl, and pour half the dressing over the salad.

3. Mix well and transfer to serving plates.

4. Sprinkle the cheese and the remaining dressing over each plate, and serve immediately.

POTATO SALAD WITH WALNUTS

A special light variation of the classic picnic favorite. You'll never have to worry about leftovers.

INGREDIENTS

Serves 4

1½ pounds potatoes, scrubbed and quartered

10 cups water

1 tablespoon coarse salt

1 tablespoon fresh basil

2 tablespoons parsley

1 clove garlic

2 teaspoons salt

1 teaspoon ground black pepper

⅓ cup olive oil

½ cup walnuts, ground

½ cup pickled red pepper, cut into strips

PREPARATION

1. Place the potatoes, water, and salt in a large pot, and bring to a boil over medium heat.

2. Reduce heat and cook until the potatoes are soft.

3. While the potatoes are cooking, place the basil, parsley, garlic, salt, pepper, and half the olive oil in a food processor with a metal blade. Process until the mixture is smooth and creamy.

4. Gradually add the remaining olive oil while processing, until the oil is absorbed by the other ingredients.

5. Transfer the mixture to a large bowl, and add the walnuts and pepper. Set aside.

6. When the potatoes are cooked, drain and transfer to the bowl with the dressing. Mix well and set aside for 1 hour.

7. After the salad has cooled, transfer to serving plates and serve, or refrigerate in an airtight container for up to 24 hours and serve at room temperature.

COLORFUL RICE SALAD

As toothsome as it is beautiful, this salad is a stunning addition to any table.

INGREDIENTS

Serves 6

1 pound colorful rice mixture (any mixture of different-colored varieties, available in natural food stores and online)

¾ cup roasted almond slivers

¼ cup scallions or spring onions, finely chopped

¾ cup roasted red peppers, finely chopped (roasted peppers are available in gourmet delis and other food stores)

¼ cup olive oil

2 tablespoons red wine vinegar

1 tablespoon salt

1 teaspoon ground white pepper

PREPARATION

1. Soak the rice in a large pot of water for at least 2 hours.

2. Discard the water after soaking, and replace the water in the pot with fresh water. (The amount should equal at least 4 times the amount of rice.) Bring to a boil over medium heat. Reduce heat and cook until the rice is just tender but still *al dente*.

3. Drain any remaining liquid from the rice, and transfer to a large bowl. Add the remaining ingredients and mix well. Set aside for 1 hour to cool and allow the flavors to mingle.

4. Serve at room temperature, or store in an airtight container in the refrigerator for up to 24 hours.

TABBOULEH WITH PISTACHIOS AND ALMONDS

A Middle Eastern delicacy, this light yet hearty salad is a great accompaniment to lamb or beef.

INGREDIENTS

Serves 4

1½ cups dried bulghur wheat (burghul)

1 cup parsley, chopped

2 tomatoes, finely chopped

½ cup roasted pistachios, coarsely chopped

½ cup roasted almonds, coarsely chopped

¼ cup olive oil

2 tablespoons lemon juice, freshly squeezed

2 teaspoons salt

1 teaspoon ground white pepper

PREPARATION

1. Soak the bulghur wheat in cold water in a large bowl for 2 hours. The wheat will swell in the water.

2. Drain the bulghur in a fine sieve placed over a bowl for 1 hour, to remove any remaining moisture.

3. Transfer the bulghur to a large bowl, add the remaining ingredients, and mix well. Refrigerate for 1 hour.

4. Transfer to serving dishes and serve chilled, or store in an airtight container in the refrigerator for up to 24 hours.

CARROT SALAD WITH CANDIED PECANS

*Candied pecans and carrots make a zesty salad with just the right combination
of sweetness, tartness, and crunchiness.*

INGREDIENTS

Serves 4

5 carrots, cut into thin,
2-inch-long strips

2 tablespoons olive oil

1 tablespoon red wine vinegar

1 teaspoon salt

1 teaspoon ground white
pepper

1 teaspoon yellow mustard

1 cup candied or sugared
pecans

¼ cup scallions or spring
onions, chopped

PREPARATION

1. Place the carrots, olive oil,
vinegar, salt, pepper, and
mustard in a bowl, and mix well.
Refrigerate for 30 minutes.
At this stage, you may store the
mixture in an airtight container
in the refrigerator for up to
24 hours.

2. Add the pecans and scallions
and mix well.

3. Transfer to serving plates and
serve immediately.

SEAFOOD SALAD WITH NUTS AND GOAT CHEESE

For this salad, use any type of seafood you like, such as shrimp, crab, or scallops.
You can even use imitation crabmeat for a tasty vegetarian salad.

INGREDIENTS

Serves 4

3 tablespoons olive oil

½ tablespoon Dijon-style mustard

1 tablespoon honey

1 tablespoon red wine vinegar

1 teaspoon salt

1 teaspoon ground white pepper

1 package salad greens

15 cherry tomatoes, halved

½ cup roasted pecans, chopped

3 scallions or spring onions, thinly sliced

½ cup croutons

½ pound cooked seafood (of your choice)

½-pound wheel fresh goat cheese, halved and sliced ½ inch thick

PREPARATION

1. Place the oil, mustard, honey, vinegar, salt, and pepper in a sealable jar. Close the jar and shake well for 1 minute. The dressing should be thick and golden. Set aside.

2. Place the salad greens, tomatoes, pecans, scallions, croutons, and dressing in a large bowl and toss to coat.

3. Transfer to a serving dish, and sprinkle the seafood and the cheese on top.

4. Serve immediately.

PASTA SALAD WITH SUN-DRIED TOMATOES AND PECANS

No mayonnaise is necessary in this delectable pasta salad variation.

INGREDIENTS

Serves 4

12 cups water

2 tablespoons coarse salt

One 1-pound package fusilli pasta

⅓ cup sun-dried tomatoes, finely chopped

⅔ cup roasted pecans, coarsely chopped

2 tablespoons olive oil

⅓ cup Parmesan cheese, grated

2 tablespoons pesto

1 teaspoon lemon juice, freshly squeezed

1 teaspoon salt

1 teaspoon ground white pepper

PREPARATION

1. Bring the water and salt to a boil in a large pot over high heat.

2. Add the pasta and reduce heat. Cook according to package directions.

3. While the pasta is cooking, place the remaining ingredients in a large bowl and mix well.

4. When the pasta is cooked, drain and transfer to the bowl with the other ingredients.

5. Mix well and set aside for 30 minutes.

6. Transfer to serving plates and serve immediately, or store in an airtight container in the refrigerator for up to 24 hours and let stand for 30 minutes before serving.

COCONUT MUSHROOM SALAD

I was served a variation of this salad in an Indian restaurant, and when I arrived home that night, I immediately attempted to recreate its delicious flavors.

INGREDIENTS

Serves 4

3 tablespoons olive oil

½ pound shiitake mushrooms

½ pound champignon mushrooms

1 clove garlic, finely chopped

⅓ cup spring onions, sliced into thin strips

¼ cup Chinese pecans

1 teaspoon sesame oil

1 teaspoon salt

½ teaspoon ground white pepper

1 tablespoon rice vinegar

1 cup coconut slivers

PREPARATION

1. Heat 2 tablespoons of the olive oil in a skillet over high heat.

2. Add the mushrooms and garlic, and cook for 5 minutes while stirring.

3. Transfer the cooked mushrooms to a large bowl, and add the remaining ingredients. Mix well.

4. Let stand for 10 minutes, and transfer to serving plates.

5. Serve immediately, or store in an airtight container for up to 24 hours and serve at room temperature.

THAI SEAFOOD SALAD

Fish sauce, or nam bplah *in Thai, is an essential ingredient in Thai cooking.*

INGREDIENTS

Serves 4

1 pound medium shrimp, cleaned

½ pound calamari rings

2 tablespoons Thai fish sauce (available in Asian groceries or online)

1 tablespoon hot chili sauce

1 tablespoon rice vinegar

⅔ cup roasted cashew slivers

2 tablespoons scallions or spring onions, finely chopped

1 tablespoon cilantro

1 tablespoon fresh basil, coarsely chopped

1 tablespoon fresh ginger, grated

1 tablespoon sesame oil

PREPARATION

1. Fill a large pot with water and bring to a boil over high heat.

2. Add the shrimp and calamari and cook for 3 minutes. Remove and transfer to a large bowl.

3. Add the remaining ingredients, except for the sesame oil, and mix well. Let stand for 15 minutes.

4. Transfer to serving dishes, and drizzle sesame oil over each portion.

5. Serve immediately, or store in an airtight container in the refrigerator for up to 24 hours and serve at room temperature.

BACON AND LETTUCE SALAD WITH WALNUTS

Crispy Canadian bacon adds a succulent smokiness to this dish.

INGREDIENTS

Serves 4

¼ cup olive oil

1 tablespoon vinegar

½ tablespoon honey

1 tablespoon yellow mustard

1 teaspoon salt

12 strips Canadian bacon

1 package romaine lettuce leaves

½ cup roasted walnuts

2 large tomatoes, cut into eight segments

1 tablespoon butter

4 eggs

PREPARATION

1. Preheat the oven to 450°F.

2. Place the olive oil, vinegar, honey, mustard, and salt into a sealable jar or container and shake well for 1 minute until the dressing is thick. Set aside.

3. Arrange the bacon strips on a baking sheet lined with baking paper.

4. Bake for 8 minutes or until the bacon is browned.

5. Place the lettuce, walnuts, and tomatoes in a large bowl and set aside.

6. Heat a nonstick skillet and cook the 4 eggs sunny-side up. Set aside.

7. Pour the dressing over the lettuce, walnuts, and tomatoes, and mix well. Transfer to serving plates.

8. Place 3 strips of bacon and one egg on top of each plate as shown in the photo.

9. Serve immediately.

BAKED
GOODS

ALMOND FETA QUICHE

Almonds and feta cheese are both common ingredients in Mediterranean cooking. The combination of flavors in this enticing quiche demonstrates why they are so popular.

INGREDIENTS

Serves 6

Crust:

½ cup butter, chilled

½ teaspoon salt

1 egg

1 tablespoon cold water

1 ¼ cups white flour

Filling:

1 egg

¾ cup heavy cream

1 teaspoon salt

½ teaspoon fresh nutmeg, ground

⅔ cup feta cheese, crumbled

½ cup almonds, crushed

¼ cup almond slivers, for garnish

PREPARATION

1. Preheat the oven to 375°F.

2. Blend the butter and salt in a food processor for 2 minutes until well blended.

3. Turn off the food processor and add the egg, water, and half the flour. Process for 2 minutes until the dough is smooth and uniform.

4. Turn off the food processor and add the remaining flour. Process for 1 minute until the dough forms a ball.

5. Remove the dough and wrap it tightly in plastic wrap. Refrigerate for 30 minutes. At this stage, the dough may be stored for up to 2 weeks in the freezer.

6. While the dough is being chilled, prepare the filling. Combine the egg, cream, salt, and nutmeg in a bowl, and whisk together until well mixed. Set aside.

7. Remove the dough from the refrigerator and transfer to a floured work surface. Roll out the dough thinly and transfer it to a 10-inch tart pan. Press the dough evenly on the bottom and sides of the pan. Trim the edges with a sharp knife.

8. Place the feta cheese and almonds in the bottom of the tart pan and pour the filling on top. Sprinkle the almond slivers on top and bake for 30 minutes.

9. Serve immediately. Store in the refrigerator for up to 2 days after baking.

WALNUT CHEESE BUREKAS

I dreamed up this recipe when I was on vacation in Turkey, after sampling some of their ingenious pastries.

INGREDIENTS

Makes 12 burekas

½ cup walnuts, coarsely chopped

½ cup cream cheese

½ cup Roquefort or other blue cheese

2 eggs

1 pound puff pastry

2 tablespoons sesame seeds, for garnish

PREPARATION

1. Preheat the oven to 400°F.

2. To prepare the filling, combine the walnuts, cream cheese, Roquefort cheese, and 1 egg in a bowl, and mix well with a fork until uniform.

3. On a floured work surface, roll out the pastry to a ⅛-inch-thick rectangle.

4. Spread the filling along the length of one side of the rectangle in a ½-inch strip.

5. Roll the rectangle into a cylinder. Cut the cylinder into 12 slices by cutting in half, then in half again. Then cut each of the four sections into 3 equal slices.

6. Arrange the slices ½ inch apart on a baking sheet lined with baking paper.

7. Beat the remaining egg and brush it on each slice.

8. Sprinkle the sesame seeds on top and bake for 15 minutes.

9. Serve immediately.

ALMOND FETA BUREKAS

Filo dough burekas are more delicate than their puff pastry cousins, which makes them slightly messier but no less delicious.

INGREDIENTS

Makes 16 burekas

½ cup roasted almonds, coarsely crushed

½ cup cream cheese

½ cup feta cheese

2 eggs

1 pound filo dough

⅓ cup butter, melted

2 tablespoons sesame seeds, for garnish

PREPARATION

1. Preheat the oven to 400°F.

2. To prepare the filling, combine the almonds, cream cheese, feta cheese, and 1 egg in a bowl, and mix well with a fork until uniform.

3. Remove 2 pastry sheets and place them on top of each other on a work surface. Spread the melted butter on one side.

4. Using a sharp knife, cut the dough into 2-inch-wide strips. Cut each strip in half widthwise.

5. Cut the corner of each piece at a 45° angle to form a triangular corner.

6. Place a spoonful of filling in the corner of each piece of dough. Fold over the corner to form a triangle. Repeat twice to form triangles of filled, layered pastry.

7. Place the burekas ½ inch apart on a baking sheet lined with baking paper.

8. Beat the remaining egg and brush it twice on each bureka. Sprinkle the sesame seeds on top, and bake for 15 minutes.

9. Serve immediately.

WALNUT CHEESE QUICHE

This heavenly quiche filled with aromatic cheeses and walnuts is a wonderful dish for a Sunday brunch.

INGREDIENTS

Serves 6

Crust:

½ cup butter, chilled

½ teaspoon salt

1 egg

1 tablespoon cold water

1¼ cups white flour

Filling:

1 egg

¾ cup heavy cream

1 teaspoon salt

½ teaspoon fresh nutmeg, ground

½ cup Roquefort cheese, coarsely grated

¼ cup Parmesan cheese, grated

½ cup walnuts

PREPARATION

1. Blend the butter and salt in a food processor for 2 minutes until well blended.

2. Turn off the food processor and add the egg, water, and half the flour. Process for 2 minutes until the dough is smooth and uniform.

3. Turn off the food processor and add the remaining flour. Process for 1 minute until the dough forms a ball.

4. Remove the dough and wrap it tightly in plastic wrap. Refrigerate for 30 minutes. At this stage, the dough may be stored for up to 2 weeks in the freezer.

5. While the dough is being chilled, prepare the filling. Combine the egg, cream, salt, and nutmeg in a bowl, and whisk together until well mixed. Set aside.

6. Preheat the oven to 375°F.

7. Remove the dough from the refrigerator and transfer to a floured work surface. Roll out the dough thinly and transfer it to a 10-inch tart pan. Press the dough evenly on the bottom and sides of the pan. Trim the edges with a sharp knife.

8. Add the cheeses to the tart pan and sprinkle the walnuts on top. Pour the filling over the top of the quiche.

9. Bake for 30 minutes.

10. Serve immediately. Store in the refrigerator for up to 2 days after baking.

BLUE CHEESE AND BRAZIL NUT STUFFED BREAD

Friends who have tasted this bread tell me that it is both unique and scrumptious. I tell them it's the ingredients, not the chef, that make it so good.

INGREDIENTS

Serves 4

Dough:

1 cup cold water

¼ cup olive oil

1 tablespoon dried yeast

3½ cups bread flour

1 tablespoon salt

Filling:

1 cup blue cheese, grated

½ cup Brazil nuts, coarsely crushed

PREPARATION

1. Place the water, olive oil, yeast, and flour in a mixing bowl. Using an electric mixer with a kneading hook, knead on low speed for 3 minutes. Add the salt and increase the speed to medium. Knead for 8 minutes.

2. Transfer the dough to a floured bowl and cover with a kitchen towel. Let stand to rise for 1 hour, until the dough has doubled in size.

3. While the dough is rising, combine the filling ingredients in a separate bowl.

4. Transfer the dough to a floured work surface and roll it out ¾ inch thick. Place the filling in the center, and roll the dough into a cylinder, like a roulade.

5. Place the dough on a baking sheet lined with baking paper, and let stand to rise in a warm place for 1 hour, until it doubles in size.

6. Preheat the oven to 425°F.

7. Bake for 30 minutes.

8. Serve immediately, or store in a cool dark place for up to 24 hours.

ONION TART WITH PINE NUTS

You can also make individual tartlets by using prepared pastry shells and dividing the filling among them.

INGREDIENTS

Serves 6

Crust:

½ cup butter, chilled

½ teaspoon salt

1 egg

1 tablespoon cold water

1¼ cups white flour

Filling:

1 tablespoon olive oil

1½ pounds onions, thinly sliced

1 teaspoon garlic, crushed

2 tablespoons fresh thyme

½ cup pine nuts

1 teaspoon salt

PREPARATION

1. Blend the butter and salt in a food processor for 2 minutes until well blended.

2. Turn off the food processor and add the egg, water, and half the flour. Process for 2 minutes until the dough is smooth and uniform.

3. Turn off the food processor, and add the remaining flour. Process for 1 minute until the dough forms a ball.

4. Remove the dough and wrap it tightly in plastic wrap. Refrigerate for 30 minutes. At this stage, the dough may be stored for up to 2 weeks in the freezer.

5. Preheat the oven to 400°F.

6. While the dough is being chilled, prepare the filling. Heat the oil in a large skillet. Add the onions, garlic, and thyme, and cook over low heat for 40–50 minutes until the onions are brown and nicely caramelized. Stir frequently while cooking so the ingredients do not burn. Remove from heat, add the pine nuts and salt, and mix well. Set aside to cool to room temperature.

7. On a floured work surface, roll the dough out to ⅛ inch thick. Transfer to a 10-inch pie pan and press down the bottom and sides. Trim the edges with a sharp knife. You can wrap the trimmings in plastic wrap and store them in the refrigerator or freezer.

8. Pour the filling in the pan and bake for 30 minutes.

9. Serve immediately.

CHEESY NUT TREATS

You can substitute the blue cheese with another favorite cheese for a slightly different taste.

INGREDIENTS

Serves 6

Dough:

⅓ cup cold water

¼ cup milk

2 teaspoons sugar

2 large eggs

1 tablespoon dried yeast

3 cups bread flour

2 tablespoons olive oil

2 teaspoons salt

Filling:

½ cup blue cheese, crumbled

½ cup feta cheese, crumbled

1 cup pecans, coarsely crushed

PREPARATION

1. Place the water, milk, sugar, eggs, yeast, bread flour, and olive oil in a mixing bowl. Using an electric mixer with a kneading hook, knead on low speed for 3 minutes. Add the salt and increase the speed to medium. Knead for 6 minutes.

2. Transfer the dough to a floured bowl and cover with a kitchen towel. Let stand to rise for 1 hour until it doubles in size.

3. Combine all the filling ingredients in a bowl, and mix well with a fork until uniform.

4. Roll out the dough on a floured work surface to a ¼-inch sheet.

5. Sprinkle the filling evenly over the dough, and roll the dough into a cylinder.

6. Cut the rolled dough into 1-inch-thick slices.

7. Arrange the slices on a greased, 10-inch round baking sheet, and set aside to rise in a warm place until they double in size.

8. Preheat the oven to 425°F.

9. Bake for 35 minutes.

10. Serve immediately.

WALNUT RYE BREAD

Rye bread has more fiber than white, but it also has a lighter texture than whole wheat.

INGREDIENTS

Serves 6

1½ cups cold water

2 teaspoons dried yeast

2½ cups bread flour

1 cup rye flour

1 tablespoon salt

½ cup walnuts, coarsely chopped

PREPARATION

1. Place the water, yeast, bread flour, and rye flour in a mixing bowl. Using an electric mixer with a kneading hook, knead on low speed for 3 minutes. Add the salt and walnuts, and increase the speed to medium. Knead for 8 minutes.

2. Transfer the dough to a floured bowl, and cover with a kitchen towel. Let stand to rise for 1 hour, until the dough doubles in size.

3. Transfer the dough to a floured work surface, and roll into a ball.

4. Place the ball of dough on a baking sheet lined with baking paper, and let stand to rise in a warm place for 1 hour, until it doubles in size.

5. Preheat the oven to 450°F.

6. Bake for 35 minutes.

7. Serve immediately.

SWISS RUSTICO BREAD

Rustico bread is traditionally Italian, but the addition of hazelnuts and raisins makes this sweet Swiss version both unique and mouthwatering.

INGREDIENTS

Serves 6

1½ cups cold water

2 teaspoons dried yeast

⅓ cup raisins

2½ cups bread flour

1 cup rye flour

1 tablespoon salt

½ cup hazelnuts

PREPARATION

1. Place the water, yeast, raisins, bread flour, and rye flour in a mixing bowl. Using an electric mixer with a kneading hook, knead on low speed for 3 minutes. Add the salt and hazelnuts and increase the speed to medium. Knead for 8 minutes.

2. Transfer the dough to a floured bowl and cover with a kitchen towel. Let stand to rise for 1 hour, until the dough doubles in size.

3. Transfer the dough to a floured work surface, and roll into a ball. Shape the ball into an oblong loaf.

4. Place the ball of dough on a baking sheet lined with baking paper, and let stand to rise in a warm place for 1 hour, until it doubles in size.

5. Preheat the oven to 450°F.

6. Bake for 35 minutes.

7. Serve immediately.

PEANUT BREAD

For a spectacular breakfast, toast this bread and top it with fresh preserves or marmalade.

INGREDIENTS

Serves 6

1 cup cold water

2 teaspoons dried yeast

1 tablespoon sugar

⅓ cup milk

3 cups bread flour

2 teaspoons salt

¾ cup whole roasted peanuts

¼ cup butter, softened

PREPARATION

1. Place the water, yeast, sugar, milk, and bread flour in a mixing bowl. Using an electric mixer with a kneading hook, knead on low speed for 3 minutes. Add the salt, peanuts, and butter, and increase the speed to medium. Knead for 6 minutes.

2. Transfer the dough to a floured bowl and cover with a kitchen towel. Let stand to rise for 1 hour, until the dough doubles in size.

3. Transfer the dough to a floured work surface and roll into a ball. Shape the ball into an oblong loaf.

4. Place the dough on a baking sheet lined with baking paper, and let stand to rise in a warm place for 1 hour, until it doubles in size.

5. Preheat the oven to 425°F.

6. Bake for 35 minutes.

7. Serve immediately.

COCONUT BREAD

To give your kids a special treat, use this bread for peanut butter sandwiches.

INGREDIENTS

Serves 6

1 cup cold water

2 teaspoons dried yeast

¼ cup milk

¾ cup coconut flakes

2 tablespoons sugar

3 cups bread flour

2 teaspoons salt

⅓ cup butter, softened

PREPARATION

1. Place the water, yeast, milk, coconut flakes, sugar, and bread flour in a mixing bowl. Using an electric mixer with a kneading hook, knead on low speed for 3 minutes. Add the salt and butter and increase the speed to medium. Knead for 6 minutes.

2. Transfer the dough to a floured bowl, and cover with a kitchen towel. Let stand to rise for 1 hour, until the dough doubles in size.

3. Transfer the dough to a floured work surface, and roll into a ball. Shape the ball into an oblong loaf.

4. Place the dough on a greased bread pan, and let stand to rise in a warm place for 1 hour, until it doubles in size.

5. Preheat the oven to 425°F.

6. Bake for 35 minutes.

7. Serve immediately.

WHOLE GRAIN PECAN ROLLS

Wholesome as well as whole grain, these rolls are great to bring to a potluck lunch.

INGREDIENTS

Makes 8 rolls

¾ cup cold water

¼ cup milk

1 tablespoon dried yeast

¼ cup butter, softened

¼ cup bran

¼ cup oats

3 cups bread flour

⅓ cup pecans, chopped

1 tablespoon salt

½ cup pecans, for garnish

PREPARATION

1. Place the water, milk, yeast, butter, bran, oats, bread flour, and pecans in a large mixing bowl. Using a kneading hook and electric mixer, knead the dough for 3 minutes on low speed. Add the salt and increase the mixing speed. Knead for 6 minutes.

2. Transfer the dough to a floured bowl, cover with a kitchen towel, and let stand to rise at room temperature for 1 hour, until it doubles in size.

3. Transfer the dough to a floured work surface and divide into 2 equal portions. Divide each portion into 4 equal portions. Flour your hands and roll each portion of dough into a ball.

4. Place the rolls on a baking sheet lined with baking paper and garnish each with half a pecan. Let stand in a warm place for 1 hour, until the rolls double in size.

5. Preheat the oven to 425°F.

6. Bake the rolls for 20 minutes.

7. Serve immediately.

HONEY PECAN WHOLE WHEAT BREAD

This recipe was inspired by a local bakery whose culinary creations were my muse for many years.

INGREDIENTS

Serves 6

1½ cups cold water

2 teaspoons dried yeast

⅓ cup honey

3 cups whole wheat flour

1 tablespoon salt

¾ cup roasted pecans, chopped

¼ cup butter, softened

PREPARATION

1. Place the water, yeast, honey, and flour in a mixing bowl. Using an electric mixer with a kneading hook, knead on low speed for 3 minutes. Add the salt, pecans, and butter, and increase the speed to medium. Knead for 8 minutes.

2. Transfer the dough to a floured bowl, and cover with a kitchen towel. Let stand to rise for 1 hour, until it doubles in size.

3. Transfer the dough to a floured work surface and roll into a ball. Shape the ball into an oblong loaf.

4. Place the dough on a greased bread pan, and let stand to rise for 1 hour in a warm place, until the dough doubles in size.

5. Preheat the oven to 425°F.

6. Bake for 40 minutes.

7. Serve immediately.

HOT
DISHES

NOODLES IN COCONUT CURRY SAUCE

A wok will make this dish easier to prepare, since its large surface area distributes the high heat evenly.

INGREDIENTS

Serves 4

12 cups water

1 tablespoon salt

1 tablespoon canola oil

1 onion, very thinly sliced

1 carrot, cut into very thin strips

1 tablespoon fresh ginger, finely chopped

1 tablespoon garlic, finely chopped

1 tablespoon green curry paste

⅓ cup fine coconut flakes

1 teaspoon salt

1 cup coconut milk

1 tablespoon soy sauce

1 package Asian egg noodles

¼ pound Chinese bean sprouts

2 tablespoons fresh basil, coarsely chopped

PREPARATION

1. Bring the water and salt to a boil in a large pot over high heat.

2. While waiting for the water to boil, heat a deep skillet or wok over medium heat.

3. Place the oil, onion, carrot, ginger, and garlic in the wok, and cook for 3 minutes while stirring.

4. Add the curry paste, coconut flakes, and salt, and cook for 3 minutes.

5. Add the coconut milk and soy sauce, and bring to a boil. Reduce the heat, and simmer for 15 minutes.

6. When the water in the pot comes to a boil, add the noodles and cook until they are soft.

7. Drain the noodles and transfer them to the wok.

8. Add the sprouts and basil, and mix well. Remove from the heat.

9. Let stand for 5 minutes.

10. Transfer to serving plates and serve immediately.

RAVIOLI WITH CHEESY NUT FILLING

When preparing this dish, be careful not to overcook the ravioli.

INGREDIENTS

Serves 4

Ravioli dough:

1 pound all-purpose white flour

6 egg yolks

2 eggs

2 tablespoons olive oil

2 teaspoons salt

Filling:

½ pound ricotta cheese

¼ cup blue cheese, crumbled

½ cup roasted walnuts, ground

1 egg

½ teaspoon ground nutmeg

½ teaspoon salt

Preparation:

¼ cup butter

12 cups water

2 tablespoons coarse salt

¼ cup Parmesan cheese, grated

PREPARATION

1. Prepare the dough. Place the flour, yolks, eggs, olive oil, and salt in a food processor with a metal blade, and process until the ingredients form a ball of dough.

2. Wrap the dough in plastic wrap and refrigerate for 1 hour. You may prepare the dough 1 day in advance and store in the refrigerator.

3. Prepare the filling. In a large bowl, combine the cheeses, walnuts, egg, nutmeg, and salt. Mix well until smooth and uniform. Set aside.

4. Roll out the dough very thinly on a well-floured work surface. You may also roll out the dough using a pasta machine.

5. Use a cup or round cutter to cut 3-inch rounds of dough. Collect the scraps and roll them out again. Repeat until all the dough is used.

6. Place a teaspoon of filling in the center of half the rounds.

7. Brush the filled rounds with cold water and cover with an empty round. Press down around the edges to seal well. Place the ravioli on a lightly floured baking sheet until ready to cook.

8. Melt the butter in a deep skillet. Set aside on the stove top to keep warm.

9. Bring the water and coarse salt to a boil in a large pot over high heat.

10. When the water comes to a boil, add the ravioli. Cook until the ravioli floats and then cook for 2 additional minutes. Transfer the ravioli to the skillet using a slotted spoon.

11. Add the Parmesan cheese and cook over high heat for 2 minutes.

12. Transfer to serving plates and serve immediately.

SCALLOPS WITH COCONUT SAUCE

Serve these succulent scallops with a light, semi-dry white wine for an unforgettable meal.

INGREDIENTS

Serves 4

2 tablespoons butter

2 pounds large scallops

1 red chili pepper, finely chopped

1 tablespoon ginger

1 teaspoon salt

¼ cup white wine

1 cup coconut milk

1 tablespoon fresh basil, chopped

¼ cup fine coconut flakes

PREPARATION

1. Preheat the oven to 400°F.

2. Heat a large nonstick skillet over medium heat. Melt the butter in the skillet. Add the scallops and cook them for 3 minutes on each side until they are golden brown.

3. Remove the scallops and place them in a baking pan.

4. Bake the scallops for 4 minutes in the oven.

5. Place the chili, ginger, and salt in the skillet, mix well, and cook for 1 minute.

6. Add the white wine and cook for 5 minutes until the sauce is reduced by half.

7. Add the coconut milk and cook for 10–15 minutes until the sauce is thick.

8. Remove from the heat.

9. Add the basil and half the coconut flakes. Mix well.

10. Divide the sauce among 4 serving plates. Place scallops on each plate, and garnish with the remaining coconut flakes.

11. Serve immediately.

BEEF WITH CHESTNUTS

*Chestnuts add richness to this unquestionably luxurious dish. Serve with crusty
bread for mopping up the delicious sauce.*

INGREDIENTS

Serves 4

½ cup walnuts, coarsely
chopped

¼ cup smooth French mustard

1 teaspoon ground black
pepper

2 teaspoons salt

¼ cup canola oil

One 3-pound slice sirloin

1 tablespoon olive oil

1 small onion, finely chopped

2 carrots, cut into ⅛-inch cubes

1 tablespoon garlic, finely
chopped

1 teaspoon ground white
pepper

1 tablespoon tomato paste

2 cups chestnuts, shelled

1 cup red wine

PREPARATION

1. Preheat the oven to 450°F.

2. Combine the walnuts,
mustard, black pepper, and
1 teaspoon of the salt in a bowl,
and mix well with a fork.

3. Gradually add the canola oil
while stirring, and mix until all
the oil is absorbed.

4. Place the sirloin in a baking
pan, and spread the mustard and
walnut mixture over the meat.
Cover the whole slice.

5. Cook for 20 minutes for
medium-rare, 5 more minutes for
medium.

6. While the meat is cooking,
heat a medium pan over medium
heat and add the olive oil, onion,
carrots, and garlic. Cook until the
onion is translucent. Add the
remaining salt, white pepper, and
tomato paste, and mix well. Cook
for 2 minutes.

7. Add the chestnuts and red
wine, and bring to a boil.

8. Cover the pan, reduce the
heat, and cook for 20 minutes
over low heat.

9. When the meat is done,
remove from the oven, cover with
aluminum foil, and keep warm for
30 minutes.

10. When the chestnuts are soft,
remove from the heat.

11. To serve, thinly slice the
meat, spoon the chestnut mixture
onto individual serving plates,
and place a slice of meat on each
plate.

12. Serve immediately.

ALMOND SHRIMP SOUP

A rich, satisfying soup made even more delicious by the addition of ground almonds.

INGREDIENTS

Serves 4

¼ cup butter

1 onion, finely chopped

1 cup blanched almonds, ground

½ cup white wine

1 teaspoon sweet paprika

1 tablespoon fresh thyme

1 teaspoon salt

1 teaspoon ground white pepper

One ½-pound can clam chowder or similar soup

2 cups water

½ cup heavy cream

1 pound fresh medium shrimp, cleaned and peeled

PREPARATION

1. Heat a medium pot over medium heat.

2. Add the butter and onion, and cook until the onion is translucent. Add the almonds and mix well. Add the wine and cook for 5 minutes.

3. Add the paprika, thyme, salt, pepper, and clam chowder. Mix well and bring to a boil.

4. Add the water and reduce the heat. Cook for 30 minutes over low heat.

5. Add the cream and increase the heat. Cook for 10 minutes over medium heat.

6. Just before serving, add the shrimp. Do not cook the shrimp for more than 3 minutes or they will become rubbery.

7. Serve immediately.

ALMOND CHILI SEAFOOD STIR-FRY

Be sure to wash your hands very well after handling the chili peppers. The oil from hot peppers can burn severely if it gets in your eyes or in an open cut.

INGREDIENTS

Serves 4

2 tablespoons olive oil

1 tablespoon garlic, thinly sliced

2 red chili peppers, finely chopped

½ cup blanched slivered almonds

1 pound small calamari, cleaned

1 teaspoon Spanish paprika

1 teaspoon salt

1 pound large shrimp, peeled and cleaned

PREPARATION

1. Heat a cast-iron skillet over medium heat. Add the olive oil, garlic, chili peppers, and almonds, and cook for 3 minutes.

2. Add the calamari. Mix well, and cook for 5 minutes.

3. Add the paprika, salt, and shrimp. Mix well, and cook for 3 minutes while stirring. The shrimp are ready when they take on an orange hue.

4. Remove from the heat and transfer to serving plates.

5. Serve immediately. Take care, this recipe tastes very hot.

WALNUT-STUFFED FISH

Serve on a bed of greens, and sprinkle some walnuts around the fish as a garnish.

INGREDIENTS

Serves 4

1 cup roasted walnuts, coarsely chopped

½ cup crabmeat

1 tablespoon + 1 teaspoon Cajun spice blend

1 teaspoon salt

1 teaspoon garlic, finely chopped

2 tablespoons olive oil

One 4-pound fresh fish, whole (snapper, grouper, or bass)

1 teaspoon coarse salt

PREPARATION

1. Preheat the oven to 400°F.

2. Combine the walnuts, crabmeat, 1 tablespoon of the Cajun spices, salt, garlic, and 1 tablespoon of the olive oil in a bowl, and mix well until uniform.

3. Arrange the fish in a heat-proof pan suitable for serving. Pour the remaining olive oil over the fish. Sprinkle the coarse salt and 1 teaspoon of the Cajun spices over the fish.

4. Bake for 25 minutes, until the flesh flakes easily with a fork.

5. Serve immediately.

COCONUT BEEF STEW

Both coconut and curry are popular ingredients in South Indian cooking.

INGREDIENTS

Serves 4

2 tablespoons canola oil

1 pound filet of beef, cut into 2-inch cubes

1 tablespoon fresh ginger

½ tablespoon garlic, finely chopped

1 tablespoon red curry paste

2 cups coconut milk

¼ cup coconut, ground

1 teaspoon salt

1 tablespoon soy sauce

¼ cup fresh cilantro, chopped

PREPARATION

1. Heat a large saucepan over medium heat. Add the oil and wait 2–3 minutes until it is hot. Add the beef cubes and brown for 2 minutes on each side.

2. Add the ginger and garlic and mix well. Cook for 1 minute.

3. Add the curry paste and mix well. Add the coconut milk, and bring to a boil.

4. Add the ground coconut, salt, and soy sauce, and reduce the heat. Simmer for 30 minutes over low heat.

5. Transfer to a serving dish, and garnish with cilantro.

6. Serve immediately with steamed rice.

ALMOND-CRUSTED WHITEFISH FILLET

Serve this delicious fish with roast potatoes or French fries.

INGREDIENTS

Serves 4

1 cup blanched almonds, coarsely ground

¼ cup fresh parsley, finely chopped

1 teaspoon fresh rosemary, finely chopped

2 tablespoons olive oil

1 tablespoon Cajun spice blend

1 teaspoon salt

2 pounds white fish (grouper, bass, halibut, or any type of white fish)

PREPARATION

1. Preheat the oven to 500°F.*

2. In a large bowl, combine the almonds, parsley, rosemary, olive oil, Cajun spices, and salt. Mix until uniform.

3. Cut several sheets of baking paper slightly larger than the fish, and place them on a baking tray. Arrange the fish on top.

4. Generously spread the crust over the top and sides of the fish.

5. Bake for 10–13 minutes, until the fish is flaky.

6. Serve immediately.

*If your oven does not reach 500°F, preheat the oven to its maximum temperature.

TURKEY ROULADE STUFFED WITH MEAT AND NUTS

Are you bored with your traditional Thanksgiving turkey but still want to maintain the turkey tradition? Liven up your table by dishing up this refreshing alternative.

INGREDIENTS

Serves 12 or more

3 pounds chopped beef

1 pound breadcrumbs

2 cups roasted pistachios, chopped

2 cups blanched almonds

3 eggs

1 tablespoon ground nutmeg

2 tablespoons salt

1 tablespoon ground white pepper

1 tablespoon onion powder

1 tablespoon garlic powder

1 tablespoon chicken soup powder

1 whole boneless turkey

PREPARATION

1. Preheat the oven to 400°F.

2. In a large bowl, combine the beef, breadcrumbs, pistachios, almonds, eggs, nutmeg, salt, pepper, onion powder, garlic powder, and soup powder. Mix well by hand until the mixture is uniform. Set aside.

3. Spread the turkey out on a clean work surface, skin-side down. Spread the filling evenly over the turkey. Roll the turkey into a roulade.

4. Wrap the roulade tightly in aluminum foil, and place on a baking sheet. Bake for 2 hours.

5. Remove from the oven and set aside to cool for 30 minutes. To store the roulade, keep it wrapped and refrigerated for up to 2 days.

6. Remove the foil and use a sharp knife to cut thin slices for serving. You may use either store-bought gravy or any other meat sauce as a garnish.

7. To serve after storing, heat the roulade in the oven for 20 minutes before serving.

LOBSTER WITH CHESTNUTS

Always buy live lobsters, or freshly frozen ones.

INGREDIENTS

Serves 4

1 pound fresh chestnuts with shells

1 tablespoon coarse salt

1 cup roasted pecans, crushed

½ cup fresh parsley, chopped

1 tablespoon fresh thyme

1 tablespoon garlic, finely chopped

½ cup breadcrumbs

½ cup butter, warmed to room temperature

1 teaspoon ground white pepper

2 teaspoons salt

Two 1½-pound lobsters, sliced in half lengthwise

PREPARATION

1. Preheat the oven to 450°F.

2. Score each chestnut with a sharp knife, arrange on a baking sheet, brush with cold water, sprinkle the coarse salt on top, and bake for about 40 minutes until the shells open and the chestnuts are hot and soft.

3. Combine the pecans, parsley, thyme, garlic, breadcrumbs, butter, pepper, and salt in a bowl. Mix well until uniform.

4. Arrange the lobsters on a pan, shell-side down. Spread a generous amount of the pecan mixture over each half. Bake for 10 minutes.

5. Remove the lobsters, transfer to a serving platter, and garnish with the chestnuts.

NUT-CRUSTED LAMB CHOPS

Since Brazil nuts have a high fat content, they do not store well. Shelled Brazil nuts should be used immediately.

INGREDIENTS

Serves 4

½ cup Brazil nuts, chopped

½ cup pecans, chopped

¼ cup parsley, chopped

2 tablespoons fresh basil, finely chopped

1 teaspoon cayenne pepper

2 teaspoons salt

1 tablespoon garlic, finely chopped

3 tablespoons olive oil

1 teaspoon ground black pepper

2½-pound rack of lamb

PREPARATION

1. Preheat the oven to 425°F.

2. Place the Brazil nuts, pecans, parsley, basil, cayenne pepper, salt, garlic, 2 tablespoons of the olive oil, and black pepper in a bowl, and mix well until uniform.

3. Arrange the rack in a pan and spread the remaining olive oil over it.

4. Use your hands to coat the sides of the rack with the nut mixture. Use the back of a spoon to press down the nuts so they adhere better.

5. Bake for 15–20 minutes. The internal temperature should read 135–140°F.

6. Transfer to a serving plate and let sit for 5 minutes.

7. Serve immediately, or store in the refrigerator for up to 2 days.

CHICKEN LIVER
STIR-FRY WITH NUTS

Chicken livers should be cooked to an internal temperature of 140°F. Use a meat thermometer to make sure the livers are cooked before serving.

INGREDIENTS

Serves 4

2 tablespoons butter

2 pounds fresh chicken livers

1 teaspoon garlic, chopped

1 teaspoon salt

1 teaspoon ground white pepper

1 tablespoon red wine vinegar

½ cup macadamia nuts, coarsely crushed

½ cup walnuts, coarsely crushed

PREPARATION

1. Heat a large heavy skillet over medium heat.

2. Add 1 tablespoon of the butter, the chicken livers, and garlic, and cook until the livers are well browned on all sides.

3. Add the salt, pepper, and vinegar, and cook for 5 minutes until the vinegar has evaporated.

4. Add the macadamia nuts and walnuts, and cook for 5 minutes while stirring.

5. Add the remaining butter, and mix well until the butter is melted and absorbed by the other ingredients.

6. Remove from the heat.

7. Transfer to serving plates and serve immediately.

BAKED
TREATS

PECAN PIE

My take on this classic recipe doesn't use corn syrup, but still tastes fantastic.

INGREDIENTS

Serves 6

Crust:

½ cup butter, chilled

2 tablespoons sugar

1 egg

1 tablespoon cold water

½ teaspoon salt

1½ cups white flour

1 egg, beaten (for brushing)

Filling:

1 egg, beaten

2 cups pecans, finely chopped

⅔ cup dark brown sugar

½ cup butter, softened

1 cup pecans, for garnish

PREPARATION

1. Place the butter and sugar in a food processor and process for 2 minutes until smooth. While mixing, scrape the sides of the bowl with a spatula as necessary.

2. Turn off the food processor and add the egg, water, and salt. Process for 2 minutes until smooth and uniform.

3. Turn off the processor and add the flour. Process until the mixture forms a ball of dough.

4. Remove the dough and wrap in plastic wrap. Refrigerate for at least 1 hour.

5. Roll out the dough on a floured work surface, ⅛ inch thick.

6. Carefully transfer the dough to a 10-inch tart pan and press down the bottom and sides with your fingers. Trim the edges with a sharp knife, roll them into a ball, and wrap the ball in plastic wrap. Store the wrapped dough in the freezer for up to 1 month.

7. Transfer the pan to the refrigerator, and chill for 15 minutes. Preheat the oven to 350°F.

8. Place a piece of baking paper over the dough, and use baking weights or beans to weigh down the crust. Bake for 20 minutes.

9. Remove the weights and baking paper, and brush the bottom and sides of the crust with the beaten egg. Bake for 3 minutes. Remove from the oven and set aside to cool on a wire rack.

10. Prepare the filling. Place the egg, pecans, brown sugar, and butter in a bowl, and mix well until smooth. Pour the filling into the prepared crust, and even it out with the back of a spoon. Garnish with pecans on top.

11. Bake for 30 minutes.

12. Remove from the oven and set aside to cool to room temperature before serving.

13. Serve immediately, or store in an airtight container for up to 2 days.

TRADITIONAL JEWISH HONEY CAKE WITH WALNUTS

Traditionally served at Rosh Hashanah, the Jewish New Year, as a symbol for a sweet year.

INGREDIENTS

Serves 4

1 cup butter, softened

½ cup brown sugar

3 eggs

1 cup honey

1½ cups cake flour

2 teaspoons baking powder

1 tablespoon instant coffee

1 teaspoon cinnamon

¾ cup roasted walnuts

PREPARATION

1. Preheat the oven to 375°F.

2. Beat the butter and brown sugar with an electric mixer at medium speed for 2 minutes until smooth.

3. Add the eggs, honey, flour, baking powder, instant coffee, and cinnamon, and reduce the speed to low. Mix until uniform.

4. Turn off the mixer and add the walnuts. Mix well with a spatula.

5. Transfer to a greased cake pan.

6. Bake for 25 minutes or until a toothpick inserted in the center of the cake comes out clean.

7. Remove from the oven, and set aside to cool completely.

8. Serve immediately, or store in an airtight container for up to 2 days.

ALMOND ORANGE CAKES

Moist and delicious, these cakes make great holiday gifts.

INGREDIENTS

Makes 5 small cakes or 1 large cake

¾ cup candied citrus peel

1 tablespoon orange liqueur (Cointreau or Grand Marnier)

6 ounces butter, room temperature

½ teaspoon salt

¾ cup powdered sugar

3 eggs

½ cup orange juice, freshly squeezed

2 teaspoons orange zest

¾ cup cake flour

½ cup blanched almonds, ground

1 teaspoon baking powder

PREPARATION

1. Grease either 5 small (4-inch) Kugelhopf pans or 1 large (8-inch) pan, and set aside.

2. Soak the citrus peel in the liqueur for 1 hour at room temperature.

3. Beat the butter, salt, powdered sugar, and eggs in an electric mixer, until the mixture is smooth and glossy.

4. Add the orange juice and orange zest.

5. If necessary, transfer to a larger bowl, and fold in the flour, almonds, baking powder, and candied citrus peel. Reserve at least 15 citrus peels for garnish.

6. Cover the batter with plastic wrap, and refrigerate for at least 2 hours.

7. Preheat the oven to 375°F.

8. If baking the smaller cakes, place 3 citrus peels in the bottom of each greased pan, and fill the pans ¾ full with batter.

9. Bake for 25 minutes or until golden brown.

10. If baking the larger cake, place all the reserved peels in the bottom of the greased pan, and fill the pan ¾ full with batter. Bake for 35 minutes or until golden brown.

11. Remove from the oven and transfer to a wire rack to cool for 15 minutes.

12. Serve immediately, or store in an airtight container at room temperature for up to 2 days.

CHOCOLATE MACADAMIA BROWNIES

Brownies are always a household favorite, and the addition of richly flavored macadamia nuts only enhances their popularity.

INGREDIENTS

Serves 6

2 cups quality bittersweet chocolate

1 cup butter

6 eggs

⅔ cup sugar

2 tablespoons coffee liqueur

½ cup flour

¾ cup roasted macadamia nuts, coarsely crushed

PREPARATION

1. Preheat the oven to 350°F.

2. Melt the chocolate and butter in a bowl set on top of a pan of boiling water or in a double boiler.

3. While the chocolate is melting, beat the eggs and sugar until foamy.

4. Add the coffee liqueur to the chocolate.

5. Using a spatula, fold the flour into the melted chocolate, and then fold the chocolate into the egg mixture.

6. Pour the batter into a 10–by–8–inch rectangular cake pan, lined with baking paper.

7. Sprinkle the nuts on top.

8. Bake for 8 minutes.

9. Transfer the pan to a wire rack to cool for 30 minutes.

10. Refrigerate for at least 2 hours.

11. Remove from the pan, and transfer to a work surface.

12. Cut into 3-inch squares using a sharp knife. Be sure to wash the knife between cuts.

13. Serve at room temperature, or store in an airtight container for up to 2 days.

COCONUT BLUEBERRY CAKE

This recipe also makes amazing muffins. Simply use a greased muffin pan instead of a cake pan, and bake for 20 minutes.

INGREDIENTS

Serves 6

1 cup butter, softened

1 cup sugar

3 eggs

1 cup coconut, ground

1½ cups cake flour

2 teaspoons baking powder

½ cup heavy cream

1 tablespoon fruit liqueur (or berry schnapps)

1 cup blueberries

PREPARATION

1. Preheat the oven to 375°F.

2. Beat the butter and sugar with an electric mixer at medium speed for 2 minutes until smooth.

3. Add the eggs, ground coconut, flour, baking powder, cream, and liqueur, and reduce the speed to low. Mix until uniform. Turn off the mixer.

4. Add the blueberries, and mix well with a spatula.

5. Transfer to a greased cake pan.

6. Bake for 25 minutes or until a toothpick inserted in the center of the cake comes out clean.

7. Remove from the oven, and transfer to a wire cooling rack to cool completely.

8. Serve immediately, or store in an airtight container for up to 2 days.

NUT MUFFINS

We baked these muffins for a charity bake sale and sold more than any other booth. Try them for yourself and don't be surprised if they disappear before your eyes.

INGREDIENTS

Makes 6 muffins

1 cup butter, softened

1 cup sugar

2 eggs

½ cup heavy cream

¾ cup roasted walnuts or other nuts, chopped

1½ cups cake flour

2 teaspoons baking powder

PREPARATION

1. Preheat the oven to 375°F.

2. Place the butter and sugar in the bowl of an electric mixer, and mix at medium speed for 2 minutes until uniform.

3. Add the eggs, cream, nuts, flour, and baking powder, and reduce the mixing speed to low. Mix until uniform.

4. Turn off the mixer and transfer the contents to a greased 6-cup muffin pan. Spoon the batter into the cups so that each one is ¾ full.

5. Bake for 20 minutes.

6. Remove the muffins from the oven, and set aside to cool completely.

7. Remove the muffins from the pan and serve immediately, or store in an airtight container for up to 2 days.

WALNUT CARROT CAKE

COCONUT CAKE

Carrot cake is one of my favorite desserts. This version is fairly healthy, but if you want to indulge yourself, top it with a cream cheese frosting.

Simple yet scrumptious, you can also frost this cake for excellent results.

INGREDIENTS

Serves 4

1 cup butter, softened

1 cup sugar

½ cup dark brown sugar

2 eggs

¾ cup roasted walnuts, chopped

1 cup cake flour

2 teaspoons baking powder

1 teaspoon cinnamon

1 cup carrots, finely grated

PREPARATION

1. Preheat the oven to 375°F.

2. Beat the butter, sugar, and brown sugar with an electric mixer at medium speed for 2 minutes until smooth.

3. Add the eggs, walnuts, flour, baking powder, and cinnamon, and reduce the speed to low. Mix until uniform. Turn off the mixer.

4. Add the carrots and mix well with a spatula.

5. Transfer to a greased cake pan.

6. Bake for 25 minutes or until a toothpick inserted in the center of the cake comes out clean.

7. Remove from the oven, and set aside to cool completely.

8. Serve immediately, or store in an airtight container for up to 2 days.

INGREDIENTS

Serves 4

1 cup butter, softened

1 cup sugar

3 eggs

1 cup coconut, ground

½ cup coconut flakes

½ cup heavy cream

1½ cups cake flour

2 teaspoons baking powder

1 tablespoon coconut liqueur

PREPARATION

1. Preheat the oven to 375°F.

2. Beat the butter and sugar with an electric mixer at medium speed for 2 minutes until smooth.

3. Add the eggs, ground coconut, coconut flakes, cream, flour, baking powder, and liqueur, and reduce the speed to low. Mix until uniform.

4. Transfer to a greased baking pan.

5. Bake for 25 minutes or until a toothpick inserted in the center of the cake comes out clean.

6. Remove from the oven, and transfer to a wire cooling rack to cool completely.

7. Serve immediately, or store in an airtight container for up to 2 days.

CHOCOLATE NUT MUFFINS

Serve these muffins as part of a buffet spread, and see how many of your guests come back for seconds.

INGREDIENTS

Makes 6 muffins

1 cup butter, softened

1 cup sugar

3 eggs

⅔ cup heavy cream

¾ cup roasted walnuts or any nuts, chopped

1½ cups cake flour

2 tablespoons fine cocoa powder

2 teaspoons baking powder

½ cup chocolate chips

PREPARATION

1. Preheat the oven to 375°F.

2. Place the butter and sugar in the bowl of an electric mixer, and mix at medium speed for 2 minutes until uniform.

3. Add the eggs, cream, nuts, flour, cocoa powder, and baking powder, and reduce the mixing speed to low. Mix until uniform.

4. Turn off the mixer, add the chocolate chips, and mix well.

5. Place cupcake liner in each cup of a 6-cup muffin pan. Spoon in the batter so each cup is ¾ full.

6. Bake for 20 minutes.

7. Remove the muffins from the oven and set aside to cool.

8. Remove the muffins from the pan and serve immediately, or store in an airtight container for up to 2 days.

PISTACHIO FINANCIERS

These French tea cakes are also known as Friands and are similar to Madeleines
in that they are both baked in molds.

INGREDIENTS

Makes approximately 25 cookies

½ cup butter

5 egg whites

½ cup roasted pistachios, coarsely ground

1 cup powdered sugar

½ cup white flour

½ tablespoon rum extract (optional)

PREPARATION

1. Preheat the oven to 375°F.

2. In a cast-iron skillet, melt the butter over high heat. Continue to cook the butter until it stops foaming and is a bright walnut color. Remove from the heat and set aside.

3. Combine the egg whites, pistachios, powdered sugar, and flour in a bowl, and whisk well until smooth.

4. Pour the butter into the batter, and mix well. This batter forms the basis for financiers. At this stage, you may add any type of flavoring you wish. When adding flavorings, begin with ½ tablespoon, and taste the batter after each addition. Be careful not to overpower the flavor of the batter or to color the batter too strongly.

5. Spoon the batter into a silicon baking tray with 1-inch-long rectangular chambers. Fill each chamber ¾ full.

6. Bake for 12 minutes or until a toothpick inserted into the center comes out clean.

7. Transfer to a wire rack to cool.

8. Serve immediately, or store in an airtight container at room temperature for up to 2 days.

BAKLAVA WITH CANDIED WALNUTS

Be sure to give the baklava a chance to absorb the syrup. Pouring the syrup on multiple times ensures that the baklava is saturated with sweetness.

INGREDIENTS

Makes 18 baklava

2 cups walnuts, finely chopped

1 cup dark brown sugar

1 teaspoon cinnamon

½ cup butter, melted

⅓ cup honey

2 pounds puff pastry

1 cup water

1½ cups sugar

1 teaspoon vanilla extract

PREPARATION

1. Preheat the oven to 400°F.

2. Place the walnuts, brown sugar, cinnamon, butter, and honey in a bowl, and mix well until uniform.

3. On a floured work surface, roll out the pastry to a ⅛-inch-thick sheet. Cut in half. Transfer one of the halves to a baking sheet.

4. Spread half the filling evenly on the pastry in the pan.

5. Place the other half of the pastry on top of the first, and spread the remaining filling on top.

6. Use a sharp knife to cut 1-inch by ½-inch rectangles halfway deep. Don't cut all the way through to the bottom.

7. Bake for 20 minutes.

8. Prepare the syrup. Place the water and sugar in a small saucepan, and bring to a boil over medium heat.

9. Remove from the heat and add the vanilla. Mix well and set aside.

10. Remove the baklava from the oven, and place on a work surface. Use a brush to coat the baklava with a generous amount of syrup. Let stand for 5 minutes and repeat until all the syrup has been used.

11. Let the baklava cool completely before serving.

12. Serve immediately, or store in an airtight container for up to 2 days.

CINNAMON WALNUT CAKE

Treat yourself to a slice of this cake with your morning coffee and enjoy the rest of the day with a smile.

INGREDIENTS

Serves 4

1 cup butter, softened

1 cup sugar

½ cup packed light brown sugar

3 eggs

¾ cup roasted walnuts, chopped

1½ cups cake flour

2 teaspoons baking powder

1 teaspoon cinnamon

PREPARATION

1. Preheat the oven to 375°F.

2. Place the butter, sugar, and brown sugar in the bowl of an electric mixer, and mix at medium speed for 2 minutes until uniform.

3. Add the eggs, walnuts, flour, baking powder, and cinnamon, and reduce the mixing speed to low. Mix until uniform.

4. Turn off the mixer and transfer the contents to a greased baking pan. Use a spatula to evenly distribute the cake batter in the pan.

5. Bake for 25 minutes or until a toothpick inserted in the center of the cake comes out clean.

6. Remove the cake and set aside to cool completely.

7. Serve immediately, or store in an airtight container for up to 2 days.

BISCOTTI

Baking these classic Italian cookies twice keeps them fresh longer.

INGREDIENTS

Makes approximately 50 cookies

3 eggs

¾ cup sugar

2 cups white flour

Pinch of salt

1 teaspoon baking powder

⅓ cup almonds

⅓ cup hazelnuts

¼ cup small raisins

PREPARATION

1. Line a baking sheet with baking paper.

2. Place the eggs, sugar, flour, salt, and baking powder in the bowl of an electric mixer with a kneading hook, and knead at low speed for 3 minutes.

3. Add the almonds, hazelnuts, and raisins, and increase the speed to medium. Knead for 3 minutes.

4. Transfer the dough to a floured work surface, and roll it into a ball. Form the ball into an oblong loaf, 12 inches long.

5. Carefully transfer the loaf to the lined baking sheet, and refrigerate for 30 minutes.

6. Preheat the oven to 375°F.

7. Bake the biscotti loaf for 30 minutes.

8. Transfer the loaf to a wire rack to cool for 30 minutes.

9. Transfer the loaf to the freezer to chill for 30 minutes.

10. Transfer the loaf to a cutting board, and cut into ¼-inch segments.

11. Arrange the slices on a baking sheet, and bake for 15 minutes at 375°F.

12. Transfer to a wire rack to cool.

13. Serve immediately, or store in an airtight container for up to 2 weeks.

MAPLE WALNUT PIE

Serve this for Thanksgiving dessert instead of the usual pumpkin pie. Top with whipped cream for extra fun.

INGREDIENTS

Serves 6

Crust:

½ cup butter, chilled

2 tablespoons sugar

1 egg

1 tablespoon cold water

½ teaspoon salt

1½ cups white flour

1 egg, beaten (for brushing)

Filling:

1 egg, beaten

2½ cups walnuts, finely chopped

⅔ cup maple syrup

½ cup butter, softened

1 cup whole walnuts, for garnish

PREPARATION

1. Place the butter and sugar in a food processor, and process for 2 minutes until smooth. While mixing, scrape the sides of the bowl with a spatula as necessary.

2. Turn off the food processor and add the egg, water, and salt, and process for 2 minutes until smooth and uniform.

3. Turn off the processor and add the flour. Process until the mixture forms a ball of dough.

4. Remove the dough and wrap in plastic wrap. Refrigerate for at least 1 hour.

5. On a floured work surface, roll out the dough to a ⅛-inch-thick sheet.

6. Carefully transfer the dough to a 10-inch tart pan, and press down the bottom and sides with your fingers. Trim the edges with a sharp knife. You can wrap the trimmings in plastic wrap and store them in the freezer for up to 1 month.

7. Transfer the pan to the refrigerator, and refrigerate for 15 minutes. Preheat the oven to 350°F.

8. Place a piece of baking paper over the dough, and use baking weights or beans to weigh down the crust. Bake for 20 minutes.

9. Remove the weights and baking paper, and brush the bottom and sides of the crust with the beaten egg. Bake for 3 minutes. Remove from the oven, and set aside to cool on a wire rack.

10. Prepare the filling. Place the egg, walnuts, maple syrup, and butter in a bowl, and mix well until smooth. Pour the filling into the prepared crust and even it out with the back of a spoon. Garnish with walnuts on top.

11. Bake for 30 minutes at 350°F.

12. Remove from the oven, and set aside to cool to room temperature.

13. Serve immediately, or store in an airtight container for up to 2 days.

ALMOND CRUNCH COOKIES

Amaretto gives these "sinful" cookies an even stronger almond flavor.

INGREDIENTS

Makes approximately 40 cookies

2 egg whites

1 cup sugar

1½ cup blanched almonds, ground

2 tablespoons white flour

¼ cup Amaretto

¼ cup whole almonds, for garnish

PREPARATION

1. Preheat the oven to 375°F. Line a baking sheet with baking paper.

2. Place the egg whites in a mixing bowl, and beat them with an electric mixer until they form soft peaks.

3. Gradually add the sugar, and continue to beat until the egg whites form stiff peaks.

4. Gradually fold in the blanched almonds.

5. Gently fold in the flour and Amaretto, and mix until uniform.

6. Transfer the mixture to a pastry bag with a ¼-inch star-shaped tip. Pipe 1-inch round circles onto the lined baking sheet, ½ inch apart. Place 1 almond in the center of each cookie.

7. Bake for 15 minutes, until dark brown.

8. Transfer to a wire rack to cool.

9. Serve immediately, or store in an airtight container at room temperature for up to 2 weeks.

COCONUT CHOCOLATE MUFFINS

These muffins taste good even when reheated in the microwave and topped with butter.

INGREDIENTS

Makes 6 muffins

1 cup butter, softened

1 cup sugar

3 eggs

½ cup heavy cream

1 cup coconut, ground

1 tablespoon coconut liqueur

1½ cups cake flour

2 teaspoons baking powder

½ cup bittersweet chocolate, finely chopped

PREPARATION

1. Preheat the oven to 375°F.

2. Place the butter and sugar in the bowl of an electric mixer, and mix at medium speed for 2 minutes until uniform.

3. Add the eggs, cream, coconut, coconut liqueur, flour, and baking powder, and reduce the mixing speed to low. Mix until uniform.

4. Turn off the mixer, add the chocolate, and mix well.

5. Place a cupcake liner in each cup of a 6-cup muffin pan. Spoon the batter into the cups so that each one is ¾ full.

6. Bake for 20 minutes.

7. Remove the muffins from the oven and set aside to cool.

8. Remove the muffins from the pan and serve immediately, or store in an airtight container for up to 2 days.

DESSERTS

PISTACHIO PARFAIT

Beating egg whites in a copper bowl always produces better results than using a plastic bowl.

INGREDIENTS

Serves 4

4 egg whites

1 cup powdered sugar

2 cups heavy cream

1 cup roasted pistachios, coarsely crushed

1 teaspoon rum

3 tablespoons roasted pistachios, coarsely crushed, for garnish

PREPARATION

1. Beat the egg whites with an electric mixer on high speed.

2. When the egg whites start to become foamy, add the powdered sugar gradually, and continue to beat until the mixture forms stiff peaks.

3. Transfer the egg white mixture to a large bowl.

4. Whip the cream with an electric mixer on high speed until it just begins to form stiff peaks.

5. Use a spatula to fold together the egg whites, whipped cream, pistachios, and rum. Mix until uniform.

6. Transfer the mixture to a flexible silicon pan (either individual serving pans or a large pan), and freeze for 2 hours. It's best to prepare this dessert 1 day in advance and store it in the freezer.

7. To serve, remove the parfait from the freezer, slice it into thick slices, and sprinkle with pistachios to garnish. For individual-size portions, there is no need to slice the parfait before serving.

SEMIFREDDO WITH CANDIED ALMONDS

Semifreddo, or half frozen *in Italian, refers to a delectable class of semi-frozen desserts including custards, ice-cream cakes, and some types of fruit tarts.*

INGREDIENTS

Serves 4

Candied almonds:

½ cup sugar

⅔ cup blanched almonds, halved

1 tablespoon oil, any kind other than olive and sesame oil

Semifreddo:

2 egg whites

1 cup powdered sugar

2 egg yolks

2 cups heavy cream

Honey or maple syrup, for garnish

PREPARATION

1. Prepare the candied almonds. Place the sugar in a heavy skillet and cook over medium heat until the sugar turns golden.

2. Add the almonds and reduce the heat. Cook until the almonds turn golden brown.

3. Spread the oil on a porcelain dinner plate, and transfer the almonds to the plate. Let stand to cool for 30 minutes.

4. Transfer the candied almonds to a food processor with a metal blade. Process until crushed. The nuts should be the consistency of breadcrumbs. Set aside.

5. Beat the egg whites with an electric mixer on high speed.

6. When the egg whites begin to become foamy, gradually add half the powdered sugar, and continue to beat until the mixture forms stiff peaks.

7. Transfer the egg white mixture to a large bowl. Beat together the egg yolks and remaining powdered sugar until creamy.

8. Combine the egg white and egg yolk mixtures.

9. Whip the cream with an electric mixer until it forms stiff peaks.

10. Add the whipped cream to the egg mixture.

11. Add the crushed almonds and combine all the ingredients with a spatula.

12. Transfer the mixture to a silicon pan (either individual serving pans or a large pan), and freeze for 2 hours. It's best to prepare this dessert 1 day in advance and store it in the freezer.

13. To serve, remove the dessert from the freezer and slice it into thick slices. For individual-size portions, there is no need to slice before serving. Garnish with honey or maple syrup.

COCONUT AND WHITE CHOCOLATE MOUSSE

Snowy white and creamy, this dessert is a pure delight.

INGREDIENTS

Serves 4

½ cup coconut milk

2 tablespoons coconut liqueur

½ cup coconut, ground

2 cups heavy cream

¾ cup powdered sugar

½ cup white chocolate, finely chopped

PREPARATION

1. In a small bowl, combine the coconut milk, coconut liqueur, and half the ground coconut. Mix well and refrigerate for 30 minutes.

2. Transfer the coconut mixture to a large bowl and set aside.

3. Whip the cream and powdered sugar with an electric mixer until the mixture forms soft peaks.

4. Use a spatula to fold the whipped cream into the coconut mixture. Mix until smooth and uniform.

5. Fold in the white chocolate.

6. At this stage, you may transfer the mousse to individual serving dishes or a large serving dish. Sprinkle the remaining ground coconut on top. Refrigerate for 2 hours.

7. Serve immediately, or store in the refrigerator for up to 24 hours.

NUT PARFAIT

Macadamia nuts make for a richer flavor, but any kind of nut will do in this sinful delight.

INGREDIENTS

Serves 4

4 egg whites

1 cup powdered sugar

2 cups heavy cream

1 cup roasted macadamia nuts (or any nuts), ground

½ teaspoon vanilla extract

Roasted nuts, ground, for garnish

PREPARATION

1. Beat the egg whites with an electric mixer on high speed.

2. When the egg whites start to become foamy, add the powdered sugar gradually, and continue to beat until the mixture forms stiff peaks.

3. Transfer the egg white mixture to a large bowl.

4. Whip the cream with an electric mixer on high speed until it just begins to form stiff peaks.

5. Use a spatula to fold together the egg whites, whipped cream, nuts, and vanilla. Mix until uniform.

6. Transfer the mixture to a silicon pan (either individual serving pans or a large pan), and freeze for 2 hours. It's best to prepare this dessert 1 day in advance and store it in the freezer.

7. To serve, remove the parfait from the freezer, slice it into thick slices, and sprinkle with ground roasted nuts to garnish. For individual-size portions, there is no need to slice the parfait before serving.

VANILLA ICE CREAM WITH CANDIED ALMONDS

This recipe requires a little extra work, but the result is well worth the effort.

INGREDIENTS

Serves 4

1 cup whole milk

1 cup heavy cream

¾ cup sugar

1 teaspoon vanilla extract

4 egg yolks

1 cup crushed candied almonds (see Semifreddo with Candied Almonds on page 112)

PREPARATION

1. In a small saucepan, combine the milk, cream, and half the sugar. Mix well, add the vanilla, and bring to a boil over low heat.

2. Whisk together the egg yolks and remaining sugar until smooth and uniform.

3. When the milk comes to a boil, pour in the egg yolk mixture gradually, and mix well.

4. Cook until the liquid reaches 175°F, and remove from the heat.

5. Pour the liquid into a clean bowl through a fine sieve in order to remove any lumps.

6. Let stand to cool completely. Cover with plastic wrap, and refrigerate for at least 4 hours.

7. Remove from the refrigerator, and add the crushed almonds. Mix well.

8. Pour the mixture into an ice cream maker, and prepare the ice cream according to the instructions and your own tastes.

CARAMEL WALNUT MOUSSE

Three different layers and textures make this mousse a sensory experience to die for.

INGREDIENTS

Serves 4

¼ cup sugar

½ cup milk

2¼ cups heavy cream

¾ cup powdered sugar

1¼ cup roasted walnuts, finely ground

½ cup butter cookie crumbs (process store-bought butter cookies in a food processor for best results)

PREPARATION

1. Cook the sugar in a small saucepan over medium heat until it becomes a dark brown caramel.

2. Add the milk and ¼ cup of the cream, and reduce the heat.

3. Cook for 20 minutes until the liquid is thick. Remove from the heat, and set aside to cool for at least 1 hour. You may prepare the sauce 1 day in advance.

4. Whip the remaining cream and sugar together with an electric mixer until the mixture just begins to form stiff peaks.

5. Use a spatula to fold together the cream and ½ cup walnuts in a large bowl. Mix until uniform.

6. Combine the caramel sauce, butter cookie crumbs, and ½ cup of the walnuts, and mix well until uniform and sticky.

7. Prepare 4 baking rings or small baking pans. Place a ¼-inch-thick layer of the caramel-walnut mixture on the bottom of each ring.

8. Fill the rings with the mousse, and garnish with the remaining ground walnuts.

9. Freeze for 1 hour. Transfer to the refrigerator for 1 hour.

10. Serve chilled, or store in the refrigerator up to 24 hours.

MARZIPAN ROUNDS

A simple but fun recipe to try with the kids.

INGREDIENTS

Makes 20 cookies

1 pound fine marzipan

¼ cup powdered sugar

½ pound organic almonds

PREPARATION

1. Place the marzipan on a clean, dry work surface, and pour the powdered sugar in a mound next to it. Cut 1-inch by ½-inch pieces of marzipan with a sharp knife.

2. Dip each piece in powdered sugar and roll into a ball.

3. Flatten each ball to ½ inch thick with your hands.

4. Make an indentation in the center of each with your thumb, and place 1 almond in the indentation.

5. Place the cookies on a baking sheet, and let stand at room temperature 30 minutes before serving.

CARAMEL-COATED ALMONDS

Better than peanut brittle and healthier too. Try this recipe with pecans and cashews as variations.

INGREDIENTS

Serves 4

1 cup sugar

¼ cup water

1 tablespoon lemon juice, freshly squeezed

2 cups organic almonds

1 tablespoon canola oil

PREPARATION

1. In a medium saucepan, combine the sugar and water, and heat over a medium flame until the water just begins to boil. Add the lemon juice, and cook until the mixture becomes caramelized and golden brown.

2. Add the almonds, and mix well. Reduce the heat to low, and cook for 5 minutes. Stir occasionally.

3. Remove from the heat.

4. Spread the oil on a porcelain dinner plate, coating it well.

5. Pour the caramel mixture onto the plate and smooth with a spoon so it fills the plate in an even layer. Set aside to cool completely. It's best to prepare the nut mixture 1 day before serving so it has ample time to cool.

6. With a sharp knife, cut the candy into ½-inch by 3-inch strips.

7. Serve immediately, or store in an airtight container away from any moisture for up to 1 week.

DRIED FRUIT AND NUT GRANOLA BARS

Take these bars with you on your next hike or camping trip, and you'll wish you'd made more.

INGREDIENTS

Serves 4

½ cup honey

1 teaspoon cinnamon

2 cups oats

½ cup whole almonds

½ cup whole walnuts

¼ cup dried cranberries

¼ cup raisins

1 teaspoon vanilla extract

PREPARATION

1. Heat a medium saucepan over medium heat. Add the honey and cinnamon, and cook until the honey begins to bubble. Add the oats, almonds, and walnuts, and mix well.

2. Cook for 3 minutes.

3. Remove from the heat, and add the cranberries, raisins, and vanilla, and mix well.

4. Pour the mixture into a deep baking dish lined with baking paper.

5. Cover the mixture with baking paper and press a heavy object (like a wine bottle) on top to tightly pack the mixture in the pan.

6. Transfer to the freezer for at least 2 hours. It's best to prepare this snack a day before serving, leaving it in the freezer for the whole day.

7. Remove the granola from the freezer, and use a sharp knife to cut 1-inch by 3-inch bars.

8. Serve immediately, or store in an airtight container away from any moisture for up to 1 week.

124

MARZIPAN ICE CREAM

Most ice cream makers allow you to specify the consistency of the ice cream, from soft to hard. You can make either type for this dessert.

INGREDIENTS

Serves 4

1 cup whole milk

1 cup heavy cream

⅔ cup sugar

1 teaspoon vanilla extract

4 egg yolks

½ pound store-bought marzipan, very finely chopped

PREPARATION

1. In a small saucepan, combine the milk, cream, and half the sugar. Mix well, add the vanilla, and bring to a boil over low heat.

2. Whisk together the egg yolks and remaining sugar until smooth and uniform.

3. When the milk comes to a boil, pour in the egg yolk mixture gradually, and mix well.

4. Cook until the liquid reaches 175°F, and remove from the heat.

5. Pour the liquid into a clean bowl through a fine sieve in order to remove any lumps.

6. Let stand to cool completely. Cover with plastic wrap, and refrigerate for at least 4 hours.

7. Remove from the refrigerator and add the chopped marzipan. Mix well.

8. Pour the mixture into an ice cream maker, and prepare the ice cream according to the instructions and your own tastes.